A One-Star Night

SONJA CIOTTI

A One-Star Night:

THE UNORTHODOX POETRY OF SONJA CIOTTI

A One-Star Night:

The Unorthodox Poetry of Sonja Ciotti

Copyright © 2015 Sonja Ciotti

All rights reserved. No part of this book may be used or performed without written consent from the author, except for critical articles or reviews.

Published by City of Oaks Books: Raleigh, NC.
Printed in the United States.

Cover Design & Illustration by Sonja Ciotti:
www.sonjaciottidesign.com

Cover Photography by Zak Ciotti

ISBN: 0692497110
ISBN-13: 978-0692497111

Library of Congress Control Number: 2015911989

DEDICATION

To my husband, Zak, the man that believes.

Let your soul stand cool and composed before a million universes.

-WALT WHITMAN

CONTENTS

Acknowledgments	i
A One-Star Night	3
On the Topic of On: A Foreword	5
On Eyewear	7
Great Horned Owl	9
Otters	11
The Czech Republic (Not to be Confused with Czechoslovakia)	12
Aberystwyth	15
Cottonwood Trees	17
C. melo	19
Honeysuckle	21
On Debating Politics and Religion: A Haiku	22
This is One of Your Favorite Things (Allergies)	23
Ants	25
The Neighbors' Dogs	27
The Mail	29
On Going to Maine, Then Not	31
Flip Flops	33
Berry Picking	34
Sitting Inside on a Summer Day	35
An Ode to That A.R. Ammons Poem I Will Never Find Again	37
Thinking a Little Bit About Swinging	39
Spider Web Demolition	41

Five Leaf Clover	43
Loblollies	44
On Being Bear Grylls	47
The Genius of Hammocks	48
Circle Back	50
Casual Fridays	52
Lake Lynn	54
The iPhone Ringtone	56
It's Never Too Late to Become the Person You're Meant to Be	58
Oo Koo Lay Lay	59
Figs	61
Farmers' Market	63
Paddleboarding	65
Drones	67
Goodberry's	69
Bees and Poetries	71
Appalachian Log Cabin	73
Quintessence	74
Shep	75
The Quail Named Jazz	77
Real Jazz	79
Why Sunsets	81
Why Big Cities are Best Enjoyed from Taxi Windows at Night	83
A London Christmas Eve	84
Soliloquy	86

ACKNOWLEDGMENTS

Thanks to Mrs. Gerstenecker, my high school English teacher who taught me about iambic pentameter and then her college-aged male teaching assistant, whose name I don't remember but most of the other girls in my class probably do, who taught me the exact same poetry stuff over again.

To my mom and dad for showing me flash cards with letters on them starting when I was aged 2 weeks; this may explain why my brain functions like a stock market ticker.

And to the kind founders and co-workers at Greenroom Communications who cheerlead my writing endeavors and encourage me to write on the Glenwood South Poetry Board, which, I regret to say, I still haven't done.

A One-Star Night

SONJA CIOTTI

A ONE-STAR NIGHT

"A Starless Night"
I remarked aloud as
The canopy overhead gave way,
Revealing the cerulean dome.

"How clever." Confident.
Certainly no other poet in the history
Of solitary star gazers
Had taken note of the dimming
Velvet curtain whisk across
Before the stars could punch
Through, one at a time
Drawing ancient, familiar shapes
Upon the tealing canvas.

How sure I could be
That although every other topic
Had been claimed one, twice, three
As if the poets formed a line
To scrape the same rake over
The same rocks
In different patterns
This one. This sky.
Was all mine.

Then, there I began to compose
The entire anthology and
The crowning jewel

The namesake
Of the whole darn thing,
An ode to all things
Natural and mysterious
Just as I
"A Starless Night."

But, the eager
The contradiction
The non observational
Observation
Stepping in on over
One declaration:
"A One-Star Night."
Interrupting my autographing
The already published classic
I looked. I saw.
One star.
So.
I tossed that classic
To start again.

ON THE TOPIC OF ON: A FOREWORD

On is one of those tiny words full of secret pomp and pageantry that academics and poets put in front of any other combination of words to make those next words sound more important. I present Exhibits A, B, and C:

"On Another's Sorrow" - William Blake
"On First Looking Into Chapman's Homer" - John Keats
"On the Beach at Night" - Walt Whitman

On means, "I have sat here in the cold, the solitude, and the wind thrashed sand blast. And I have thought about the subject you are about to read whilst drinking your herbal tea, cuddled up with a Nate Berkus throw from Target, for at least twice as long as you will probably ever sit or think about any single subject. As long as you live."

That is what most poets mean by On, anyway.

I just like to sort of ironically ride the coat tails of On's air of importance and apply it only to those subjects that no one would ever otherwise find all that important. I wouldn't mind if I found out one day a group of highly educated literary critics gathered together around some swanky Manhattan loft, book in one hand and glass of pinot noir in the other, to analyze to death the next poem in this book "On Eyewear," just because the On made the Eyewear seem worthwhile to analyze.

Mostly, I use On just because I like the sound of it. On. And it's little. Like me.

For fear that you'll soon think this has turned into some sort of hybrid prose and poetry experiment or something, I will hijack your poetry reading no longer.

On to enjoying yourself while reading poetry.

Cheers,
Sonja

ON EYEWEAR

Since giving up
The public display of
Purple plastic spectacles
A score or so ago
There is hardly a soul
Who once knew
And even hardlier a soul
Who remembers
That I see daily
Through contortion.

I, too, forget
Until the nightly ritual
The eyes sacrificed
Like peeling away
Strange fish scales
Carefully placed
In sterile bowls
And I take up my blindness
As a weary cane
Directly where I left off
In the morning.

Again, in the shower
A rogue sud, sliding down
Burning
And it is then I consider

Perhaps the blind man
Healed by Jesus
Wasn't that blind
Rather, Jesus
Was the first optometrist.

GREAT HORNED OWL

After the usual nighttime routine
The toothbrush slipped back in its slot:
A stiff, upright sentinel glistening
After fighting the good fight.
Wistfully spying the empty slot
Temporarily vacated
By his vanity comrade.

And now the Hollywood-style filaments
Bursting like supernovas then
Cooling to eerie embers
Turning on the lonely afterlife.
Curtains sealed against the moonlight
Suddenly every footfall
A wary extension into the abyss.
Hands stretching vulnerably
To bump the comforting bedpost.

Silence.

Then.

Somewhere beyond that dark veil
Who who who? Who who?
Demanding answers
A spine-tingling question
For a solitary sleeper.
A deep, direct question:

Who?
Asked not once,
But five times!

Jumping upright
The sentinel
Peeling the curtains
Moonlight cascading
Are you up? Me too.
Nose to the glass,
Is it you?
The empty branches clattering
Breathlessly cerebrating
Who? In return.

OTTERS

Why do they roll
Upon the open swells
Of this closed confinement
Touching the sterile glass
Of their manmade boundaries
With the softness of
An outstretched bounce
And why do they collect
The tiny stones
Like the once hard hearts of
Their onlooking counterparts
Who are far more free
And hold them to their chest
And keep them for their own
And finally, why do they clasp
The hand of their neighbor
Just before their eyes close
For the scheduled night
Carried softly by the
Artificial current
Under the painted sky, covered
With acrylic stars
When no one else is looking
If not to remind us?

THE CZECH REPUBLIC (NOT TO BE CONFUSED WITH CZECHOSLOVAKIA)

For some it was memorizing the scripts
Of all three- now six- soon nine- Star Wars
Or conquering Sonic the Hedgehog
Level by level, whatever that means.
But for me, it was twisting the globe
Round and round and
Tapping an intriguing spot that
No one had heard of,
At least not on this side of the sphere,
Then, learning all I could.

Now psychology researchers call it
Epigenetics: the ancestral remembrance
Progenitors' memories
Get stuck in your blood
And swirling through your mind
And pulsing through your desires
Is the itch to return
To where your DNA once roamed.

But all I knew is that something
About the sound of the language:
The palletized letters, the rolling r's
The accent on every starting syllable,
The imagination that every girl
Wore a soft silken scarf
Covering her head

And a neat embroidered apron
At her waist,
And the sound of the music,
Well, Dvořák took me there
The proud horns blaring
In minor chords
Slavonic Dances and The New World.

I dreamed of it for years
The 2D postcard of imagination
Of gothic spires and gray smoke
Frozen in the sky
But then I stepped out of the postcard
And into a taxi, headed for Malá Strana
On a glorious, golden evening.
The soft, sweet breeze on my cheeks
Rustling the red white and blue
Not Stars and Stripes but
Triangles and Trapezoids
Fluttering from the red roofs
Late summer in Prague!
Winding down the hill
Listening to the sound of
Familiar birds chirp against
The unfamiliar rhythm
Of the cabby's friendly chatter.

And my heart swelled with 3D rapture
And stamped a spot on the passport
Of my soul.

Hand hanging out the window,
Riding on the air,
Just like back home
But here
Bouncing down cobblestone streets
And losing count of the bridges
As they piled up on the horizon
Finally, to find myself
In the Czech Republic.
Not to be confused with Czechoslovakia.

ABERYSTWYTH

Aberystwyth, you old friend.
You started out a fictional place.
No more real than Atlantis
Or Middle Earth.
Or more specifically,
You could have been Middle Earth
For all I knew.
And still could be.
I read along the curve of your
Misting, gray shore
I read the way you greenly
Sloped down from two points:
The Camera Obscura perched
On one side and
The Pen Dinas fort
On the other.
I read that you met regally
In the middle at
The National Library and
Casually walked the Promenade.
But I didn't read about
The way the wind whips around
Your pastel rainbow of town homes
(The green one of which, my heart
Has already moved into
And neatly unpacked all its socks)
Or their tidy, uniform dormers
Peering out to sea,

Like friendly amphibians
Never blinking
Keeping watch over
The flags of all those nations
Flying wildly inland.
I also didn't read about
The way all those y's sound
Or all those consonants
For that matter
The way the young
Fiercely grasp this seminal language
The world fell asleep to centuries ago.
Also, could anyone have ever
Captured the words for me
To read about the
Heavens carving holes
Straight through the grey
(Not gray)
Billowing mass
And sending cylinders of sun
Dancing like daytime spotlights
Alighting patches of sheepy green
And sparkling sea alike?
So, that all of my senses
Would have resonated
As one
That this one
Corner of the earth
Was carved out
Just for me.

COTTONWOOD TREES

Everyone recalls the byproducts
Of an oddly warm winter
We smile
And shake our heads
At the daffodils sending their shoots
Up through the December frost
And we dare to imagine
The blooms will follow
Knocking at our door, early
In their tropical print shirts,
Tanned, golden
Towing their stamped suitcases
As welcomed Christmas guests.
Those premature blades
Sending up a reminder
Like a natural telegraph, signaling
Earth in her bounty
Will spring forth again.

And when she does
We ride on bicycles through life
At blazing speed
Senses filled with verdancy,
Sweat dripping like rain.
Dogs panting under the sun.
Life has just started!
And we are immortal!
Then a cloud of white

Breaks off from the Heavens
And falls, falls slowly enough
So we can get a good look
At this tiny snowball lookalike
Though carrying the seeds
Of the next generation
Still sending down a reminder
Like a natural telegraph, signaling
Before we close our eyes.

C. MELO

On paper
It has the makings
For a match made
In Heaven with me.
Enormous emerald
Elephant ears hiding
The low viney connection of
Bulbous netted treasures:
A summertime delicacy,
The peachy cream crescent.

But instead, it is the fruit
Equivalent of that
Pandora song-
The one you continuously
Skip over and over
And Pandora never learns
Or possesses an ulterior motive
And keeps serving it to you,
Sure you weren't in your
Right mind
The last time you tried it.

It wouldn't be so bad
If a fresh slice
Didn't already smell
Like yesterday's refuse
And who can forget

That a worldwide search
For the moldiest object
On earth
Led researchers
To its bin in a market
Where the prize winner festered.

So, when I discover
The seasonal fruit
On the menu is
Not berries,
Not citrus,
But a bowl of these
Cool fleshy chunks
I just close the menu,
Return it to the waiter,
And ask for a different season.

HONEYSUCKLE

These are the golden days of spring
Golden rays after six and the
Sweet, juicy floral filling the yard with
Notes on a vine: ivory, canary, gold.
If scent were a sight this early night
Surely there would be a honey drop
Dripping off the sun, low in the sky
Unusually low, touching
The tongues of innocent youth,
An endless soft trumpet to travel down,
And fuzzy knots at the end of taut ropes
Tossed out, still, in the air.

ON DEBATING POLITICS AND RELIGION: A HAIKU

Don't, don't, don't,
Don't, don't.
No, really.
Don't.
Let me think about it:
Nope.
Don't.

THIS IS ONE OF YOUR FAVORITE THINGS (ALLERGIES)

Remember how Alanis Morissette
(And no, until this moment
It had never occurred to me
I might find myself
Scribbling a verse on her)
Sang of rain on wedding days? and
You mouth the words: A free ride
Before I even ask
The next question.

If that melody continued on
For another handful of verses
We might have eventually
Heard the tale
Sung of my little sister
Her little white room
With the purple curtains.
Lincoln Park lyrics
Sweetly embroidered and
Hanging at her door.
And then the horses.
Horses on the walls,
Horses on the shelves,
There's a book, no
A horse,
No a book about horses.
And a dream to one day

Ride free into the sunset
A single rider, a single horse.
And then train all the horses.
But.
The day came
The scheduled first encounter
The first sneeze
Two, three
The closer the horse stamped,
Wagging its tail
The more violent the sneezing.
And so, little sister
You had to return to your room
And your horses' heads hung low
To bear up the weight
Of all of our
Antithetical dreams.

ANTS

To me
They are just the dots of life
Earth moving underfoot
Forging a razor line,
Uncannily reminiscent of
The traffic trudging along I-40.
A carving through broccoli trees
From my airplane window.

To you
They are the deliverers of terror
Created solely for
The diabolical mission
Of infesting your bags, your cot
Even your sleeping bag
No longer sacred
To the creeping horde.

What if
Your story began instead
On the edge of a frosty snow field
Void of the teeming mass
To set up your first camp
In your polar fleece
And your subzero sleeping bag
To brave a different bite?

There silently

Sleeping under the icicle stars
A velvety trail of crystals
Exhaled into the Heavens
As you blissfully slept
Unbothered, indeed unaware
Of the existence
Of crawling life.

But then
What if the suffering were inevitable?
What if instead of ants, yaks?
The massive herd, stamping
Maniacal glint in their eyes
Cots, sleeping bags
The snow flailing tumult!
The uproarious camp!

I don't know
If this turn of events would have
Radically shifted your life's course.
Navigating you carefully around
The yaks of the world, not ants.
But if such a detour
Meant our paths wouldn't cross
I thank the Heavens

For ants.

THE NEIGHBORS' DOGS

Pugs.
From the Latin word Pugnus
Or "fist"
Or "handful"
(So far all of this is accurate).

Each morning they awake
And I don't believe they
Consciously consider
What havoc they might wreak
In the lives of their owners and
Associates that day
Instead, it appears
They were programmed overnight
By some paranormal force
Maybe the Lord of the underworld
And with the rumbling we hear
Through our thin walls
That's the sole explanation
Drums of the dog demons
Lifting these two creatures
Upon their backs
With fire in their cockeyed glares
To meet the day
In ruthless pursuit of
Every squirrel and
Harmless neighbor girl
Growling with rage

At the meaningless restraint
Their doggy harnesses attempt
To inflict upon them.
Rage against the grass
Rage against the trees
Rage against a sudden wind
But not against the fireflies
- That's just fear -
And when their rage loses muse
At last they turn on one another
Brothers at birth, but now
Seeing each other in a new light
Inevitable foes, the gladiator match
Bitterly ensuing blow for blow
Until they are returned to
Their underworld caves for the night
To start it all afresh
Tomorrow.

THE MAIL

Many a prospect has floated
Through its romantic gears
Stamped sifted sorted
And then delivered
By the local celebrity
Who could be seen
Approaching for miles in
Those shorts and those socks
Pulled up yea high, yea
The bearer of gifts,
The granter of dreams
To those of us who waited
Impatiently for that
Signed baseball we had to
Choke down all that cereal for,
To those of us teenagers
Whose star crossed loves
Wrote from the other side
Of the world
Or the next county over -
It was all the same when we
Owned no license nor car,
And to the almost
High school grads we were
On whose
College acceptance letters
Hung the balance of our future
Opportunities to explode with

Exponential growth
And perform an inverse reaction
In our moms' and dads'
Bank accounts.

I suppose the magic continues
Into adulthood
Now we wait impatiently
For those Michael Kors bags
We bought on eBay From China
Because obviously that
Is going to be legitimate
Or the love letters addressed to us
From anonymous companies
Myriads of mysterious suitors
Courting us
With the prospect of two free
Round trip tickets to an exotic
Destination of our choice
If only we'll only call now!
Or the good news from the
Credit card companies
That we have been accepted
To enjoy a low introductory rate
A whole new world of
Spending power, with
Exponential opportunities
To buy more Michael Kors bags.

ON GOING TO MAINE, THEN NOT

Yes, I admit once before
I'd crossed the bridge
Over from Portsmouth
And immediately I downshifted
To a more comfortable pace
"The way life should be"
Graciously greeted by
The contently hanging rainbow
Of Lobster buoys
Warren's low shack full
Of their job well done
On the other side.

As I said, I've been there once
And anyone who knows, knows
Visiting once is like
Eating once, breathing once
You get the picture
About once.

So.

I bought the tickets!
In a flurry
The flight, the hotel, the car
All arranged
Already packed, unpacked
Already standing on our little deck

Overlooking the harbor
The fresh fishy air
Toy boats racing
Over glimmering swells
The anticipation of joining them
Tomorrow playing at
The corners of my mouth.

But.

I'd bought refundable tickets.
That's the problem.
For refundable tickets are
An invitation to the cosmos:
Come! Interrupt! Ruin my plans.
One word from the cosmos:
Gladly.
One by one
The flight, the hotel, the car
Falling off the edge of that little deck
Overlooking the harbor
And waving the toy boats
Goodbye.

FLIP FLOPS

They're an onomatopoeia
And that's fun and all
But the fun stops there.
Who enjoys
The conspicuous flip
The deafening flop
While trying to walk
Through life's echoing hallways
To get to the place
Where no one will take you
Seriously wearing those
Two boogie boards
Haphazardly held on
By thick canvas straps
Designed with just the right
Coarseness to inflict
Maximum blister action
To that part you once liked
Or at least could ignore
Between your toes?

BERRY PICKING

Remember when we dug through
The mud, the sludge
Uncovering nothing but roots
Leading straight down to the source
That we didn't want to directly view?
What grew in the abysmal void?
Unable to let go,
We kept digging and digging

Until

Somehow a ray poked through
Shining over your head in our selfie
The lake behind us smooth as satin,
Heavy and solid as gold
And the peaches and roses
Stretched out overhead
Like a childhood blanket.
It was there we found along the shore
Low to the ground: nature's polka dots
Bunches of fuchsia and indigo morsels
Dropped upon her verdant petticoat.
At first we picked for ourselves
Then we picked for each other
The breeze slowed to a whisper
And the sun knowingly beamed down
As we found
What we were digging for.

SITTING INSIDE ON A SUMMER DAY

If my calculations are correct
In this neighborhood alone
I am missing out on at least
Forty four barbecues firing up
To grill those hand pressed patties
Meat juice dripping down to sizzle
On the smoking coals
And fifty three front yards
At any given time
Hissing as their sprinklers spray
Concentric arcs of city rain
Back back back and
Forrrrrrrrth
Conjuring a rainbow mist
Of extraordinary luck to every kid
Who manages to ride her bike through
Necessarily holding her breath
And (this is the most important part)
Reciting silently the alphabet
In reverse.
I suspect I may also be deaf to the sound
Of three thousand ice cubes
Clinking the bottom of sweating
Sweet tea glasses, cheering
To another slice of the
Seedless melons, locally grown
And the grand finale
The backyard spectacle of

A hundred thousand, give or take two
Bioluminescent floaters
Rising up from the brush to twinkle
In chaotic synchronicity
And, not to be outdone,
Their non-lighted cousins
Going out in a blaze of glory
All their own
Zap!
Yes, that's certainly
More excitement
Than I'm having.

AN ODE TO THAT A.R. AMMONS POEM I WILL NEVER FIND AGAIN

At once I remembered
A stray poem I'd gathered up
Long ago, I'd tucked it
In my ruby satin heart pocket
With the others
And every once in a while
I'd take it out, each time
The bluing ink fading
Encouraging me to store it
In the place where
Poems don't die.

But, life
And all of its forgetting.
Until I felt the lining, the hole
And tripped over the shoelaces
Of its absence
I sent out the search party
Flashlights in hand
To seek the burgundy edges
And the jade block platform
From which the Art Deco font jumped
When I last remembered seeing it.
But it doesn't help
That I first started searching
Through e.e. cumming's work
To find this tiny verse

That was probably already
Shorter than this poem
Currently is.

Even now all I can remember
Is that plane overhead
Flying somewhere, maybe Rio?
And every time I see
A silver vessel
Its shining sides reflecting
The lowering sun
A trail of Heaven mist
Streaking the sky
I wonder how far
Those lost words have traveled
By now.

THINKING A LITTLE BIT ABOUT SWINGING

I like words
That sound just as they are
Swing
I can almost feel the hands pulling me
High up into the air and
-ing
The rush of downward thrust
Hair flung into the sun

And I like the motion
Of pumping legs
Swing
And straightening out again
-ing
Back and forth
Going absolutely no where
Yet the preferred method
Of transportation
For all 4-year-olds

The dismount, though
The true measure of bravery
To time it at the highest point
And risk certain death?
Swing
Or to wind down

Lightly scraping mulch
Until the earth itself
Stops spinning?
-ing

We were molded
Into who we became on those
Scorching rubber seats
The risk takers,
Swing
The cry-babies,
-ing
Forged of competition
Sometimes in unison
Sometimes oscillating
All pushing
The limits of natural laws
The squeaking chains
Warning us they are all
That keep us tied
To this world.

SPIDER WEB DEMOLITION

Oh, arachnid.
When you spent that hour last night
Weaving back and forth
Up and down and through and over
One tedious line at a time
Did you have visions of
Cornucopious feasts at midnight?
The webby dew goblets all
Glistening and filled to the brim
By morning?
A toast to the delicacies
All flying about now
But spinning slowly
On the rotisserie by brunch?

Did you build in that particular spot
Because the view is to die for?
The wall of cascading honeysuckle
Spilling onto the lush green carpet
Beneath you
Well, I can't argue with your taste
Seeing as it is my own back deck
But seeing is not what I did
When I plowed straight through.

The cornucopia upturned!
The goblets smashed!
The rotisserie desecrated!

And all of a sudden I was
An accidental god
Wreaking havoc on your world
And teaching you a lesson,
Which I see this evening,
You clearly didn't learn.

FIVE LEAF CLOVER

From my lofty tower
I gaze down upon the massive throng
Of indistinct green clusters I see
The forest rather than the trees
One shag carpet someone kindly
Rolled out before me.
But others with the accuracy
And the same persistent hunting
The eagle motions sweeping down
And clenching tight within their grasp
And plucking up sweet victory
Those peculiar oddities
Nature sending up its question marks
About the laws it should obey
What's one more leaf?
Ten thousand to one
Cheerfully explained away.
Then I heard the other day
The altogether poignant news
Not one extra leaf, but two
And now I fear I can't decide
Whether to clap my hands
And chuckle aloud about
This lucky world in which we live
Or pack my bags and hide underground?
How do we know we've gone too far
When nature refuses to comment
Except for this five leaf clover?

LOBLOLLIES

Secretly
I anticipated our annual meeting
When my family and I would pack up
The mammoth silver van
Brimming with Sunbelt snacks
And other sustaining rations in tow
And we would start down the country road
Into the sleepy early morning rays
Headed for the nearest shore,
Which wasn't very near,
But when one lives as a dot
On the endless sentence of the prairie
One knows well the un-nearness of all.

And I would jump in the very back
Flinging open those gray velvet curtains
Such a luxurious perk of the nineties
And I would let the world outside
Zooming by at seventy miles an hour
Filter through my senses
Rows of corn funneling towards the clouds
Seamlessly transforming into rolling hills
I couldn't tell when the black soil
Gave way to the red clay, but never mind
I kept a vigilant watch for my greeting party
The first tall pines.

And when I spotted them, I knew

It was much more official than those
Welcome to Kentucky signs with a horse
Warning all to buckle up in this state
Or else
Theirs was the natural sign:
Friendly, waving
Welcoming me South.

Those pines.
The magic of collinear trunks grouped
Together like a tidy box of pencils
I wanted to preserve unsharpened
Leading up to the sparse clouds of
Blue-green needles that fell into
A bouncy burnt sienna carpet
I could have spent all afternoon
At that rest stop picnic area
Warming in the baked pine scent
But there's never enough time
Rolling by at seventy miles an hour
Towards the sea.

Fast forward
Now
And between each letter I am reminded
So close, I could run out to meet them
I glance up from the ease of my windowsill
Over a saturated summer scene
Outlined against the nine o'clock sky
My guardians on the horizon

The collinear trunks, the cloud needles
Have you been waving the entire time
Welcoming me home?

ON BEING BEAR GRYLLS

He once said he can't imagine
The millions of people
With their two millions of eyes
Glued to him while he leaps
Plummeting like a stick figure
In a physics diagram
Rocks and debris tracing
The dashed trajectory lines
Of another escaped death.

What must he think about
On the way down?
"Did I brush my teeth this morning?"
That's what we're wondering, anyway.
Maybe for him, practical thoughts flow:
"Is it cold? Will it hurt?"
"Do I have the right materials to splint
A broken femur? Or two?"
Or perhaps no fully formed thoughts
Perhaps an abstract collage
The blur of green and brown and white
A familiar tickle of a thrill
Closing in on the strange simplicity
Of the horizon between
This life and the next
And hoping, as we invisibly hope
He lands on the right side
Again.

THE GENIUS OF HAMMOCKS

I imagine it went like this:
The first person stood
Thinking simple thoughts
Between two trees
Staring down at the leaf-laden ground
Shifting up to the hushing canopy
And deciding aloud, "I could sleep
Somewhere between here and there."

And thus a lifestyle was born
The ultimate in luxurious repose
The declaration: this is my afternoon!
And I will spend it in this solitary sling
Eyes closed, gently rocking
Listening to the birds warbling
Improvising a composition about
How they already thought of this
Years ago
But I am content to catch up
On all the thoughts
I've been meaning to think
Like how the Royal Family is doing
And did they enjoy their tea on the lawn
Amongst the perfect pointy hedges
This June afternoon?
Furthermore
Who will win the French Open?
And here again it circles back

To royalty
If Roger is still king
And Serena still queen
Surely I've got all the time in the world
To take up my own royal post
Ruling dutifully over this suburban shire
As long as my throne can be
This lazy lingering hammock.

CIRCLE BACK

Before we all go drinking the Kool-Aid
I think we first need to consider
The implication of too many cooks in the kitchen
Preparing their snackable, low-hanging fruit,
Or worse yet, anything vanilla.
Why don't we just let it all simmer
Until the dream team hits the ground running
Synergizing game-changers in their wheelhouse.
Their core competencies and alignments
Had better be laser focused and bleeding-edge
Because, frankly, at this price-point,
I don't know how much of a buy-in we can expect.
It would take a visionary to induce
A real paradigm shift in our influencers,
Engaging them with best practices and
Empowering them to internalize solid corporate values.
This is our window of opportunity, though,
To drill down and achieve as much leverage as possible.
I think we've got the bandwidth
And all of the moving parts to make this happen.
So, do you want to reach out, or shall I?
I know our chief shareholders have been out of pocket
For some time now,
But I think we can capitalize
By circling back with them via an e-blast.
Or we can definitely just put a pin in it for now
Until we get our ducks in a row, because we've been
In the weeds, failing to make hay or yield results.

In conclusion,
Let's think outside the box and braindump
To devise an innovative solution.
Because at the end of the day
It is what it is.

CASUAL FRIDAYS

Thank you.
Thank you for allowing us
To free that top button and throw off
Those sharp black heels
Which would otherwise be clanking
Down the cold marble halls
At the end of this week.
How lucky we are you decided
This last HR meeting
To consider our comfort
To allow for it once a week, anyway.
So here I sit
Plaid nylon capris rubbing,
Squelching against the leather grain
And I see Bob through my window
Fiddling with his polo
And brushing his Bermuda shorts
Awkwardly exposed
As he can't make eye contact
With upper management
Whose interpretation of casual involves
Armani suits and crocodile loafers.
He reminds me a little
Of that tattooed smoker
In his best Sunday chaps
Chains at his hips jangling a bit
As he nervously shifts his weight
Gazing around at all the suited men

From the back of the church
The sign out front did say
"Come as you are."
Right?
The both of them contemplating
The exquisite discomfort
Born of the invitation
To be comfortable
And the homelessness that comes
With racing thoughts
Maybe I can change
Maybe I will be a better man
On Monday.

LAKE LYNN

I studied some local maps
I dusted my bike, oiled the gears
Then off I set, field book in tow
To document this canopy land
Where colonists settled four centuries ago
And when I arrived at the spot I gazed
At the well-trimmed dome-like grassy hill
And figures casually walking its spine
Like tightrope walkers against the sky
Obscuring any hint of the treasure behind
The gray paved trail leading the way
Up above the silver rippling ribbon
That beckoned to every duck and goose
And a blue herring, creeping, teetering
Down into the cool shaded coves
And over long stretches of boardwalk
Skimming the noon day sparkles
Pushing up the fishy breeze
Upon which the turtles relax.
And that was it.
I'd found my spot.
I carefully laid out my picnic blanket
To stake my claim on a front row seat
So that in her reflection I could see
The spectacle of changing leaves
Giving way to quiet barren branches
Then the first courageous blooms
Pushed over by gregarious green

And in her reflection I see me
A little younger than the day before
More alive, anyway
This is her daily healing spring
Given forth so freely
At Lake Lynn.

THE IPHONE RINGTONE

Ah, the staccato rain
Those eighteen drops
So effortlessly
Bouncing one by one
Down our auditory canals
From the line in Au Bon Pain
To the shuffling taxi streets.
Is it just one person or two?
Tap tap tapping at that marimba
Aggressively, for those who
Like that sort of thing
And cheerfully, for all the rest.
Lilting the accidental
African or South American
Masterpiece
That actually required
Years of research
You know, the stereotypical
Scientists in white coats
Hooking up all sorts of wires
To all sorts of brains
Determining
That this frequency
Of this instrument
In this note pattern
Picked at the brain
In just a way to induce
Maximum response

Maximum attention
Maximum status
And now we're all Pavlov's Dogs
Salivating at the sound
Or reaching for our pockets anyway
Because those eighteen drops
Could be beckoning
Any one of us.

IT'S NEVER TOO LATE TO BECOME THE PERSON YOU'RE MEANT TO BE

That's the extent of a euphemistic meme
Circulating the boards of thirty-somethings
Who make bucket lists
And make to-do lists
Never to-do

We are all now watching life through screens
The lives of others on sprees
Of living life once
You only live once
Hashtag this

Don't go anywhere without documenting
If you don't get tagged you'll be lamenting
That you're not Friends
So the Friends of Friends
Can envy you

Maybe real life doesn't happen anymore
At least not the way it happened before
When the dew and the dogs and the dreams
The person you scheme to be and the dreams
Were all private

OO KOO LAY LAY

We steam across the heartland
In a rusting train's caboose
Moonlight leading the way
On the rails
Clattering the nostalgic rhythm
Of a bygone era.

Or sometimes I don
My satin flapper dress
With the long knotted pearls
He does his best Louie Armstrong
And together we croon
Love songs in French
Drenched in roses and the moon.

But most of the time
I take him home
Where he is called by his real name
Where the sand is bathed
In moonlight and stars
And the ocean's white caps
Roar against the obsidian night
And we lean against the nearest palm
And we sing about whatever he likes
Love, mostly
Calypsoing more, thinking less
Even his minor chords - friendly
Daisies springing up through the mud

And when I pick them,
He sings.

FIGS

Now there's a pretty little fruit
Those ovoid ornaments dangling
Like drips of dark, earthy marsala
Trickling from the tree of life
Beckoning passerby to pick them
Just to feel firsthand the striking sensation
Of the cool, refreshing curves
Meant to fit in the palm, just so
Skin to skin
And to revel in the delicate reverence
Of this ancient muse.
Even Samuel anthropomorphized
The regal orchard dweller
Along with his peasant neighbors
Recounting a seminal conversation
When the other trees begged
That the fig might rule over them
And in his inherent demureness
The fig declined this promotion
Content to keep the simplicity
Of his tender bounty unsung.
So instead I will sing
Or at least hum a little tune
About the joy of the subtle spicy pulp
Like a globe's molten core spilling out
Under the shade of the plenteous lobes.
And I would gladly paint
Its subtle hues in dewy plump strokes

If only I could paint
So I'll simply gaze
Until the golden rays wash the day away
And distill dew droplets
On all those smiling faces.

FARMERS' MARKET

There's something promising
About summertime Saturdays
To wake up with the dew
The brewing yellow sky
Threatening her sunny showers
Thirteen boxes on the calendar
To fill up with Earth's plenty
So, let's try it again
Let's drive to the massive bustle
Cars swarming like frenzied bees
Converging on the hive of Raleigh.
Who cares how far away we park?
This time we'll stroll, unhurried
That is, until the rush descends,
And we're swept into the natural flow
Down the buzzing, crowded corridor
Cash waving in the air as we recall
Our cards are no good in these parts
Starting with the expert pie makers,
Swiftly shoveling their glorious goods
Chocolate chess and blueberry lime
Into snapping plastic clamshells,
Sliding down the checkered counter
We'll be back to catch our own
But we just remembered
Our appointment with the next table
Where we'll take our sweet time
Sampling each open jar of fruit

Arranging our very own
Amuse-bouche a la saltines
And suddenly we are connoisseurs
Of all things jam: traffic and toe and
The flow moving us along; we'll return
But we've got goat cheese!
Too bad no one's stopping
Not even us
Because there's soda across the way
Prickly pear and birch beer
And Cheerwine in clear glass bottles
Which everyone knows is better.
Should we buy here? Wait; there's more
Out the door, across the way
Another bustling corridor
This one bursting at the seams
With buckets of rainboweous bounty
Rows and rows of stalks and stems
Roots and leaves and buds and blooms
And plastic forks peddling mid-air
Juicy samples of every kind
Like a grand finale of flora and fruit
Erupting at once in identical lots
But the flow comes to an abrupt halt
We said we'd come back
And push our way like trout upstream
Instead we are led gently back to our car
Inevitably, once again
Empty-handed.

PADDLEBOARDING

It's no wonder Matthew and Mark
Enthusiastically recounted that time when
Jesus stepped out of the boat
And uprightly walked on water
As enthusiastically as gospel writers
Could manage, anyway
Without having felt the thrill themselves
Of the first wobbly, fluid step
Then steadying, balanced
One foot in front of the other
Gliding majestically over glass
And suddenly the horizon was no longer
The trap door into which
All natural creatures fell
But now a gleaming, solid superhighway
Across which a standing man could travel
In a sharp line cutting straight through
The perfect roundness of this fish bowl
And he could look up at the Heavens
The clouds so crisp against the blue
Whisking by as if in a hurry
To tell their Maker that man has joined them
And he could look down at the watery abyss
An aerial view of the swirling fish dance
Stirring up the swells in pursuit of food
And each other
Refusing to make eye contact
With this new, unnatural, looming shadow.

And he could reach out his hand
Beckoning his friends to join him
Visions of spending a timeless day together
Coasting these uncharted waters
And knowing what I know now
It's strange only Peter took up the offer
Carefully placing the first wobbly, fluid step
Straight through the trap door
Did his friends laugh?
Did he fear the deep?
Did he hate getting wet?
What I always wanted to know was
How the story would end
If he had got himself up
Steadied himself
And tried once more.

DRONES

One day, said the news
We might be out toiling in the garden
Sweat beading under our straw hats
From plucking out of the soil those pesky weeds
And tossing their dirty, exposed roots
Like circuits ripped from the motherboard
Into a pile of refuse
And looking up in the blinding noon
We will hear the familiar buzz
Of a harmless foe
And we might even nonchalantly swat at it
Just to drive home the point
Of how clueless we will be
That the buzzing
Has come to deliver our mail
Or pick up our dry cleaning
Or deliver our Starbucks
And we will set aside our garden spades
As the buzzing patiently hovers
Even technology will wait for a tip
Now, no more an awkward glance, a cough
An outreached hand of a uniformed bellhop
Now just the brazen stare
The cold tinted glass dome eyes
Hiding all the ones and zeros
Of its directive
To deliver our dress shirts today
But tomorrow to return and survey

You know,
Just for enhanced mapping purposes
And if it happens to snap a shot of our speed
As we pull out of our driveways
Barreling down the street in our Teslas
Well, that saves a policeman
The menial task of sitting in wait
Just for us
He is freer now
And isn't that a marvel
Look at all the freedom we'll gain
From the buzzing keeping track
A watchful eye on our daily whereabouts
Noting we bought Brussels spouts
And passed up the asparagus
Each little tidbit a stored one, a zero
Buzzing overhead us
As we toil in our gardens
Sweat beading under our custom tailored hats
From plucking out of the sky those pesky bees
And
Crunch
Tossing their sterile, exposed wires
Circuits ripped from the motherboard
Into a pile of refuse.

GOODBERRY'S

When the sweet heat
A hazy dream puddle
Shimmers across the concrete
And when the bloodgoods turn
Burgundy into ripening cherry
And even when a brisk chill
Swirls the caramel crisp leaves
Round and round the parking lot
This little joy spot keeps a light on
A string of lights in fact
And wrapped around the framing foliage
Twinkling like Grandfather's eyes
Welcoming all of his children home
To sit a while and reminisce
Or at least chat about things as light
As the whipped cream topping
On the featured sundae
Young and old alike, yes
All his children gather to
Giggle again and again
At the clever trick
The way the concrete
Can be flipped
Upside down
Spoon and all
That never gets old.
Such a simple selection
A single flavor of the day

All befitting the seasons
A raspberry drop sliding down
And sizzling on the pavement
A touch of maple almond bundled and
Cozy together under the bloodgoods
And the snowy eggnog field folded into a cup
Brilliant white against the cold, starry night
Somehow melting together all generations
Into perpetual innocence
And spoon savoring youth.

BEES AND POETRIES

They seem to attract one another
Like Bonnie and Clyde
Or more like the bees are
Both Bonnie and Clyde
And the poetry
Is that nice family man
They ran off the road
While living riotously
Drunkenly seeking out
Their next thrill
Their next sting.
All the while the poetry
Begs to be written
Just one more word!
Maybe one more line
Before it's forced out
Of its wicker seat
To turn out all its pockets
Empty all the gold and
The wisest gems
That were so legitimately earned.

Well, no more.

I am the posse, come to
Rain terror on these troublemakers
And put an end to the torture
Of those innocent words.

I mount my stance
Armed with enough ammo
To light up a vespa village
And watch all of their hiding places
Curl inwards, forcing them out
Blinking blindly into the sunlight
Sparks raining down and bouncing
Just once
As silence falls
Over the still smoking scene.

But, armed not, as it turns out
With a frore enough heart
I lower my artillery,
Buzzing now immutable,
And me and the poetry
Slip indoors.

This time.

APPALACHIAN LOG CABIN

Autumn's slowing golden rays
Descend quietly like russet leaves,
Framing a quaint pretty forest box
Of tidy match sticks
White matches
To be specific and stacked
Just so
Their burnt black ends overlap
And their fire engine shutters sway
To the forest's piney sigh
And somehow the heart aches
For the simplicity of such an outpost
The proverbial four corners
And roof over one's head
With just enough room to
Strike the matches
And coax that swirling smoke spire
Up the drawing brick column
Shaking our hair back from our eyes
With a wink of pride
At having mastered this primal labor
Made a little easier than our ancestors had it
By premade fire in a wrapped brick
But never mind that
We might as well have invented fire
At this point
Our newfound curiosity, unblinking
A flame curling and softly crackling
Around these gathered logs.

QUINTESSENCE

A soft sole placed
On this wild earth.
A soft soul placed
Into tender hands.

SHEP

So let it be written
That upon the records of the canine kingdom
Over which he ruled for a mighty decade
He was known as Schaeperkoetter of Shoal Creek
The territory over which he governed
Or marked, anyway
Stretched far and wide across the grassy prairie
And Shetland sheepdogs just as far and wide
Envied his flowing, dark locks
Trailing him like a perfect motion blur
As he trotted down the lawn,
An A-list Hollywood star.
But to us, he was just Shep
The fury of energy that jumped up
To meet his nose with a little girl's hand outstretched,
Who had no patience for those stupid
Obedience games
Like the hotdog on the nose
No
Because hotdogs tasted too good
And likewise no interest in playing fetch
Since he quickly calculated
The one-sidedness of this so-called game.
But he understood the value
Of patiently letting the little girl
Open up his mouth -wide- to study his teeth
And reach in
To see how far his tongue went back there

Because that was just anatomy practice
And because all too soon
The little girl would go off to school during the days
And the house would grow too silent
What's a dog to do
In the invisible boundaries of the kitchen floor
And only the sound of his own clawed paws
Tap tap tapping as he paced
With no one to chase
Or lick
But alas
When the sound of the car's engine
Rumbled back down the driveway
And with a swift car door slam
The girl ran to meet him
Well, no sweeter of a reunion could there have been
Each and every afternoon.

THE QUAIL NAMED JAZZ

Those tiny eggs
So out of place
Like smooth river stones
Washed up on the shore
Of our garden
Now motherless and
Utterly exposed
Their only hope
To catch the eye
Of a fatherly farmer
Who might scoop up
Their war torn nest
To place them inside
The glowing electric womb
And wait to see
If an omelette
Or a baby hatched
In time
In a few days in fact
One lone egg
Sent out a little tremor
Tipping the world over
And one molten lava crack
From the core
Started to spread
Across the surface
Helped by the mini
Pick axe tapping

Crack crack crack
Until she was free
To sing her first notes
Doo dee da dee
Da dee doo
"So what" you ask
But "So What"
Is the answer
Her seminal chirp
A Miles Davis classic
And thus
Jazz was born.

REAL JAZZ

Does not conjure images
Of waiting in a dentist's chair
Gripping the tan pleather arm rests
Or the awkward metallic railing
Tracing the tiny perimeter of this elevator
And especially not the Doppler radar
Moving across large swatches of the country
In repeating colorful rotations
Eight minutes past the hour, every hour
On The Weather Channel.

No, you'll know it
When you hear it
Feel it
See it
Suddenly the lights will dim
Into high contrast blue in green
And a low rumble will emanate
From somewhere below
Perhaps stools scraping the stage
Or the bass tuning up up up
Like the ribbon of smoke coiling
From the cigarette left at the edge
Of a shadowed music stand
And the counting will commence
A-one, pause, two, pause
A-one, two, three, breathe
Life into fractal notes

The rain of the piano splattering
Upon the heartbeat of the bass
Conjuring steam from the winds
Their abstract chords billowing
Picasso clouds that caress the rafters
And the farthest chair in the back
Now rolling on the wave of
The trumpet's authoritative entrance
Only to be outdone in cool confidence
By that crooning tenor sax
And by this time
All ears hang on to the lifeboat
Of the notes
Swelling like chaotic visions
Of season-free storms
Finally winding down
This Birdland scene
At three o'clock in the morning.

WHY SUNSETS

For the record
Sunrises are equally magnificent
The same lilac stain under
A fluffy peach veil
Obscuring that inobscurable
Celestial orb
Radiating like nothing else
Like itself
Located on this side of the sky
Rather than that
But, let's be honest
Sunrises rank number two
Simply due to the fact
That they're far too early.
Sunsets, however;
Timed to perfection
In the winter to draw us home
Just before the porch lights switch on
With their vacant stare and we're a
Stranger in our own homes. No.
Rather, we arrive just in time
To wrap a blanket around our
Shivering shoulders
And stand at our windows
With the satisfaction of the
Fading light falling on all that is ours.
And timed so perfectly
In the summer to draw us out

To enjoy the lingering rays
Maybe a walk around the golden lake
To sense the heat's descent
And journey until bed
To dream of the cicadas' song
And the gently waving trees
Dropping sweet shadowed acorns
To bring our attention to
The creeping caterpillars underfoot
Changing colors ever so
Imperceptibly, quietly
Much like this fading sky.

WHY BIG CITIES ARE BEST ENJOYED FROM TAXI WINDOWS AT NIGHT

Because the night is young
And so are we.
Donning our long dresses
And freshly pressed coat tails
This anticipatory ride swells
Up and down these gritty hills
Past the glitz of neon barbecue
And hotel stars and guitars
Fusing with the stretched red glare
The heavy taillights creeping along
Like the nondescript bystanders filed
Around a corner and down the block
Shuffling civilly to keep warm and
Turning in one chilly breath as we pass.
Outside our muted, lustrous glass
Downtown bokeh dots aglow
Like a shower of everycolored jellybeans
Silently pouring outside our windows
Until we roll those windows down
To shrill sirens over rumbling sounds
Wide-eyed, we reach out our hands
And leave our own strobey streaks
To capture any colored moments we can
Leaving none for the pursuing caravan
Since
It's all for our taking
Tonight.

A LONDON CHRISTMAS EVE

There's a second floor walk up
Nestled just so above the lilting crowd
Flipping their collars against the
Chill winter gust
Whipping the corners of
Carved flourishes in cool concrete
Maybe it's located at 221B Baker Street
Or one of those other flinty stoops
That crisp wind whipped us right along
So I really can't be certain where
But I did carefully detail
The way the early setting sun
Would enter in through the front room
Its final embers sweeping the fireplace
And setting off the blaze
Beneath the knitted striped socks
Weighted by ancient leather books
Keepers of all that history and even
The scent of pipes and a hint of earl gray
Fused into dark mahogany
Framing the windowsill's settled snow
In each of the tidy five o'clock quadrants
As five chimes distantly toll
The kettle's on and whistling its first notes of
Away in a Manger
(The British version, of course)
And soon all of our friends will
Arrive to carol and carry on

In jolly animated tones
Around the flickering twinkle lights
Draped upon the fresh cut Yule.
But until then
A quiet toast
To the simplicity of
This toasty scene
This winter dream
Schemed by you and me.

SOLILOQUY

Why do I type here
In my first floor
Suburban study
On a sunny, summer
Afternoon
With the windows
Open and closed
At the same time?
Don't they say something
About God closing a
Door to open a window?
Anyway, it might as well
Be true
For when I glance up
I notice again the printed words
In pink and gold foil
"the future is bright"
As if God wrote them
In his own friendly handwriting
And the angels that I know
And the angels of the postal service
Placed them safely in the mailbox
For me to carefully open
Like a nest housing a baby bird
I wanted so tremendously to live
The roughly drawn flourishes
Still pointing outward
To another time

But for now
I'll set one last blaze
Gathering together
Like kindling,
Memories
Like tinder,
Tears and
Laughter.

ABOUT THE AUTHOR

Sonja Ciotti's poetry career started in 1993 when a poem about a sunset she wrote as a fourth grader from rural Illinois was chosen as an official selection for a youth poetry anthology. Indeed, a poet was born. It wasn't until she was much older and wiser (so probably in sixth grade) that she realized that the work of every one of her fourth grade classmates who wrote a poem had been included in the anthology as well. Too late; the fourth grade spark ignited a lifelong love for reading and writing poetry. In her undergraduate studies, Sonja minored in English and earned a Bachelor of Arts in Psychology. She continued on to earn her Master of Science degree in Marketing and currently works in the field of marketing and advertising, specializing in branding and graphic design. But in the quiet moments, Sonja can be found jotting down her poignant and humorous life observations, patching them together in the most beautiful artistic medium - the written word. She lives in Raleigh, North Carolina, with her husband, Zak.

www.ingramcontent.com/pod-product-compliance
Lightning Source LLC
Chambersburg PA
CBHW020946090426
42736CB00010B/1290